# On Planet Earth

Author Paul Mason
with artwork by Mark Ruffle

WAYLAND
www.waylandbooks.co.uk

First published in Great Britain in 2018
by Wayland
Copyright © Hodder and Stoughton, 2018

Series editor: Paul Rockett
Series design and illustration: Mark Ruffle
www.rufflebrothers.com

HB ISBN 978 1 5263 0576 3
PB ISBN 978 1 5263 0577 0

Printed in China

Wayland, an imprint of
Hachette Children's Group
Part of Hodder and Stoughton
Carmelite House
50 Victoria Embankment
London EC4Y 0DZ

An Hachette UK Company
www.hachette.co.uk

# Contents

# Cause and Effect

What is 'cause and effect'? It is the connection between two events, when the first event leads to the second.

One way to explain cause and effect is through examples.

### Cause:
Your cousin loves singing along to pop songs. This causes her to ...

### Effect:
... sign up for an audition on a TV talent show.

The effect of this could be that she becomes the new Queen of Pop!

## But cause and effect doesn't always work out well ...

Because she always wears headphones, your cousin hasn't realised that she can't actually sing.

The effect is embarrassment all round.

4

# In the big processes on planet Earth, though, cause and effect can sometimes lead to chaos!

Sunshine causes hot, damp air to rise up into cooler air and form clouds.

Wind begins to spin the clouds, which rise higher and higher, forming a supercell storm.

The supercell unleashes heavy rain, hail, thunder, lightning and tornadoes.

Hot, damp air

Chaos!

# The Big Bang

Planet Earth is an amazing, complicated, beautiful place. It's filled with roaring oceans and raging rivers, monstrous mountains and parched deserts.

But how did the Earth come to be here in the first place?

It all started with a big bang. In fact,

## THE Big Bang.

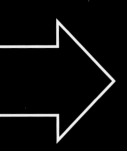

The Big Bang scattered matter throughout the Universe.

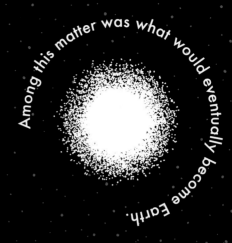

Among this matter was what would eventually become Earth.

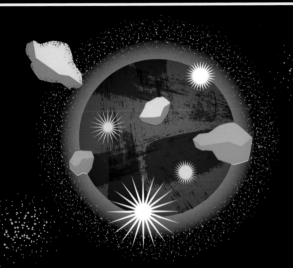

The start-up Earth had enough gravity to attract more matter, in a process called

## accretion.

Once Earth had reached a certain size, it began to cool on the outside. The cooling-down created a hard shell, or crust. Beneath the crust was molten matter.

As far as scientists know, out of millions of planets in the Universe only Earth supports life. Imagine if things hadn't happened just as they did ...

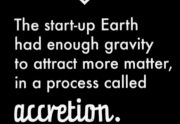

... our 'air' might have been *poisonous gas* ...

... the 'ground' might have been **molten rock** ...

... or the oceans might have been *boiling hot!*

7

Planet Earth's outer crust isn't in one piece like an egg shell. It's made of several pieces – more like a boiled egg you accidentally dropped.

The pieces are called tectonic plates. Where they meet, volcanic eruptions can happen without warning.

— Tectonic plates

**Tectonic plates** are constantly on the move. Sometimes their edges move together.

The magma rises, forming a volcano: a hill of rock with a magma chamber beneath.

magma

Plates only move a few centimetres each year.

One plate is forced beneath the other.

Hot rock under the upper plate turns into magma: molten rock.

When the pressure inside gets too great, the volcano erupts.

# Chaos!

Over time, gases build up in the magma chamber, like a shaken-up fizzy drink.

When Mount Vesuvius erupted in CE 79, it **destroyed** the ancient Roman cities, Herculaneum and Pompeii.

# Birth of an Island

Far out in the Pacific Ocean are the Hawaiian Islands. They are 3,750 km from North America and 6,400 km from Asia. It's a long way to the nearest continent.

The Hawaiian Islands did not float away from one of these big landmasses – so how did they get there?

Hawaii started life at a 'hot spot': a place where hot matter from deep within Earth rises close to the outer crust.

**Sea level**

**Hot spot**

**Ocean floor**

Scientists think hot spots may be a cooling system for Earth's core.

The hot spot is below the ocean's tectonic-plate floor. When it gets especially hot, it melts the plate. A volcano is born, deep beneath the sea.

The volcano rises up and up, until it bursts out at the ocean surface, 5 km above.

Mauna Loa, on Hawaii, is the world's tallest volcano:

*it is over 9 km high in total.*

With its heat released, the volcano-making eruption stops – until next time.

By then, the Pacific plate will have moved.

*A new island will be formed.*

Hawaii's volcanoes are still *active*. They regularly erupt.

Lava flows across roads and through fields ...

buildings are destroyed ...

and clouds of ash coat the land.

# Earthquake!

Mid-afternoon on 22 May 1960 in Valdivia, Chile, the ground started to shake in a violent earthquake. The city's people evacuated their buildings – but it was just a foreshock.

Thirty minutes later, the biggest earthquake ever recorded struck Chile. What had caused it?

## South America

Valdivia, Chile

South American Plate Boundary

Nazca Plate Boundary

The earthquake began off the coast, where two tectonic plates were grinding against each other.

Instead of gliding smoothly, the edges of the plates had become stuck.

The **tension** between the plates kept increasing. Finally, they began to release, causing a series of foreshocks.

Tension

Tension

South Atlantic Ocean

South Pacific Ocean

The shockwaves spread out from the epicentre like ripples on a pond. They were felt hundreds of kilometres away.

Epicentre

shockwaves

The loosened tectonic plates lurched violently into new positions, causing a giant earthquake.

In Chile, thousands of buildings were so badly shaken that they collapsed. Two million people lost their homes. Many people were injured or died.

There were many **landslides.**

JAM

The foreshocks loosened the plates – like when you hit a stuck jam-jar lid and make it easier to open.

Whole towns shifted suddenly to the west – by as much as **nine metres.**

13

# Tsunami!

On 26 December 2004, people living or visiting countries along the Indian Ocean noticed the sea level suddenly go down. Some knew what it foretold: a tsunami was coming.

The tsunami began with an earthquake, deep below the ocean.

**The waves travelled across the ocean at over 500 kph.**

Out in the deep ocean the waves were barely noticeable, less than 1 metre high.

The pulses were like the waves in a sheet you quickly flap up and down repeatedly.

A 1200-km long section of tectonic plate under the Indian Ocean had suddenly moved. The earthquake pushed up the ocean water above.

**Gravity pulled the water down again. This fast rise and fall sent pulses of movement across the ocean.**

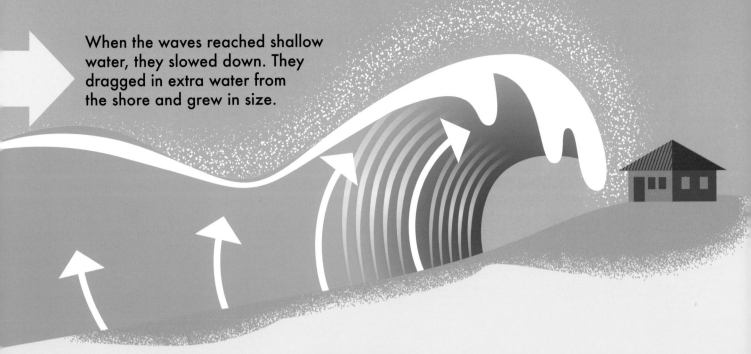

When the waves reached shallow water, they slowed down. They dragged in extra water from the shore and grew in size.

In places the tsunami was **30 metres** high when it crashed onto land.

Around the Indian Ocean, the tsunami uprooted trees, smashed houses and threw boats inland. In total, roughly a quarter of a million people are thought to have died.

15

# Flash Flood!

In Cornwall, UK, summer rain is not unusual. On 18 July 2017, though, it began raining especially hard. Then hailstones big enough to smash windows began to fall.

For the village of Coverack, things were about to get even more extreme. A flash flood was on its way.

Hours before, thunderstorms had formed over the warm sea. Their warm air contained a lot of **moisture.**

The wind blew the storm clouds towards land.

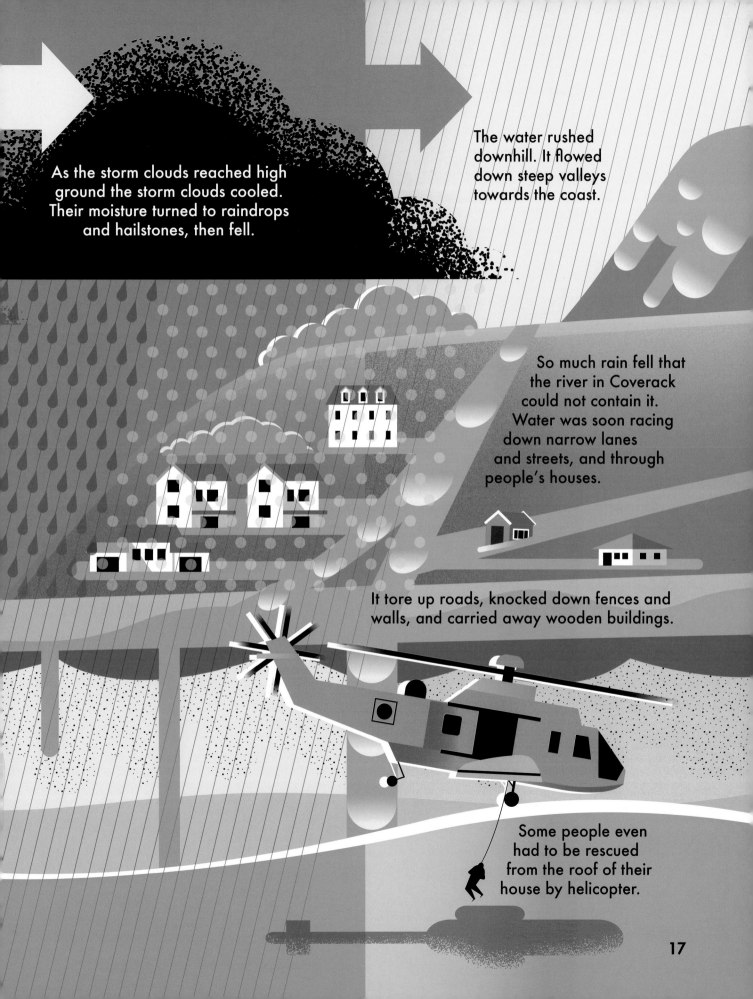

As the storm clouds reached high ground the storm clouds cooled. Their moisture turned to raindrops and hailstones, then fell.

The water rushed downhill. It flowed down steep valleys towards the coast.

So much rain fell that the river in Coverack could not contain it. Water was soon racing down narrow lanes and streets, and through people's houses.

It tore up roads, knocked down fences and walls, and carried away wooden buildings.

Some people even had to be rescued from the roof of their house by helicopter.

# Avalanche!

In Afghanistan in February 2010, avalanches swept across the Salang Pass road to Kabul. One hundred-and-sixty-five people were killed.

**The avalanches,** like almost all others, had been caused by a combination of snow and warm weather.

As winter begins, **snow falls** on the high mountains.

If the sun comes out and the temperature gets warmer, the top layer of snow melts and becomes water.

On the cold ground the snow does not melt. It piles up wherever the land is flat enough. Sometimes the snow piles up above a steep slope or a cliff.

When night falls and the temperature drops the watery layer freezes. It turns into ice.

When more snow falls, it lands on slippery ice instead of *grippy ground.*

Eventually, so much snow falls that it all slips off the icy layer below.

# Avalanche!

The avalanche races down the mountain, collecting more snow as it goes. It also collects mountaineers, trees, ski lifts, skiers, houses – anything in its way.

# Hurricane!

On 26 August 2017, Hurricane Harvey hit Texas in the USA. Within days, 50 people were dead and there was a trail of destruction wherever Harvey had been.

Harvey – like all hurricanes – had started life over an area of warm ocean water.

As more and more air rushes in, the storm grows increasingly powerful.

By the time it has become a hurricane, it may be 15 km high and big enough to see from space!

Warm water vapour rises to form clouds. The clouds grow taller and taller.

Warm water vapour

Down below, more air rushes in to replace the rising air. It swirls around, warming up and rising in its turn.

**Category 1:**
119–153 kph winds

**Category 2:**
154–177 kph winds

**Category 3:**
178–208 kph winds

# Hurricane Harvey

**Category 4:**
209–251 kph winds

**Category 5:**
252+ kph winds

When a hurricane reaches land, warm ocean water no longer powers the swirl of rising air. It slows down.

The hurricane's giant clouds release their water. Hurricane Harvey dropped over a metre of rain on parts of Texas.

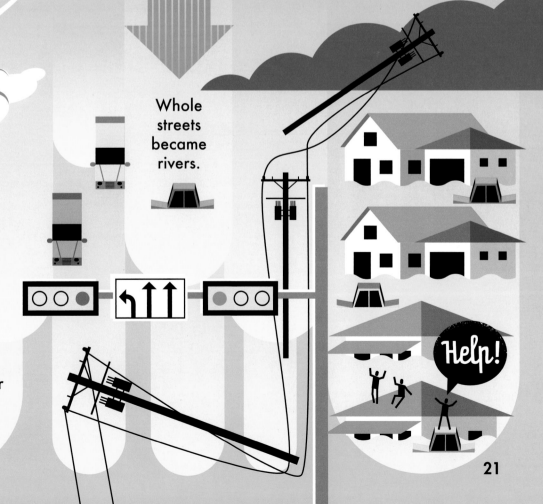

Whole streets became rivers.

Some people took refuge on rooftops.

Others were rescued from their flooded homes.

Help!

# Water Pressure!

For tens of thousands of years, Aboriginal Australians have been travelling across their country's parched deserts. They survived because they knew about springs where fresh water mysteriously appeared at the surface.

The water's story had begun millions of years ago – when dinosaurs still walked the Earth.

Back then, Australia's sandstone rock was covered by a layer of waterproof rock.

Mountain rain began to sink below ground and into the sandstone. It spread out, but could not rise to the surface. Every time it rained, more water was pushed underground.

Waterproof rock

Sandstone
(not waterproof)

Later, an edge of the rock was pushed up by the movement of tectonic plates, forming the Great Dividing Range of mountains.

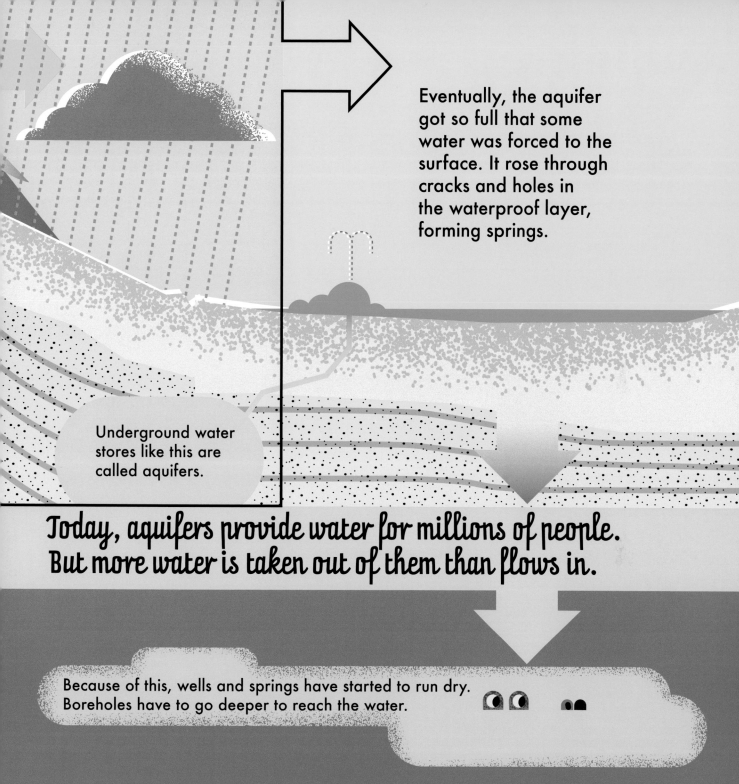

Eventually, the aquifer got so full that some water was forced to the surface. It rose through cracks and holes in the waterproof layer, forming springs.

Underground water stores like this are called aquifers.

Today, aquifers provide water for millions of people. But more water is taken out of them than flows in.

Because of this, wells and springs have started to run dry. Boreholes have to go deeper to reach the water.

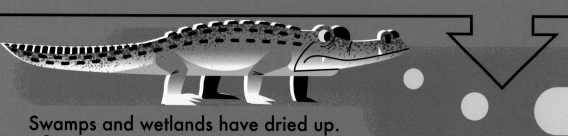

Swamps and wetlands have dried up. This is a disaster for the creatures who live here.

# Wildfire!

Almost every year in the USA, thousands of Californians are forced to flee their homes because bushfires are headed their way. When they return, some find only the smoking shell of their house.

The fires are among thousands that spring up around the world every year, often in late summer and autumn.

Wind pushes the fire towards more dried-up vegetation. A line of flames called a 'fire front' forms.

Bushfires are started by lightning, sparks from rockfalls, dropped cigarettes, barbecues and a range of other causes.

The heat of summer dries out the plants and soil.

Something starts a fire among the dried-out plants. The flames grow higher and trees begin to catch light.

Heat from the fire front dries out the trees and plants ahead.
They release flammable gases and burst into flame.

Hot air

Oxygen

Hot air from
the fire front
rises. Colder
air is pulled in,
giving the fire
fresh oxygen
to burn.

**Animals**
are affected too
– and even after
the fire, survivors
are at risk from
dehydration.

Now the fire may rage for weeks. It will destroy thousands of
homes, and anyone caught in the fire's path will lose their life.

# When the Sea Eats the Land

Lennox Island is off the coast of Canada. Lennox is small – and getting smaller. In 1880, it was 615 hectares in size. Today it is 500 hectares.

Like coasts around the world, Lennox Island is being eaten away in a process called coastal erosion.

Out at sea, a storm appears.

The waves travel towards the shore. When they reach shallow water, they rise up and start to break.

## Wind blows across the surface, forming waves.
The longer and stronger the wind blows, the bigger the waves become.

# The waves crash against the coast, smashing down rocks and sand.

In places where the land is soft and earthy, it is washed away like a sandcastle in a rising tide.

Where the land is rocky, the water attacks by forcing air into cracks in the rock, making them bigger and splitting the rock.

Air

The land above suddenly has nothing holding it up. It collapses into the sea.

Sometimes lighthouses, gardens or even people's houses fall into the sea too.

# Overheating Earth

Earth is getting warmer. In 2016, the average temperature was 0.9°C (1.69°F) warmer than the average from 1900–2000.

Warmer temperatures may sound like a good thing – but they are actually having a chaotic effect on planet Earth. And what's worse is that humans have caused them.

Between the 1960s and today, the world's population more than doubled.* Industry, agriculture and other human activity also increased.

 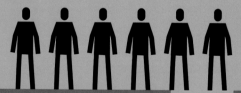

Human activities produced gases called greenhouse gases, which were released into the **atmosphere.**

Since 1960, the amount of greenhouse gases we release has gone up by nearly 30 per cent.

greenhouse gases

Atmosphere

The greenhouse gases joined a layer high in the sky, which traps heat in the atmosphere.

28

*From roughly 3 billion to 7 billion.

Earth's average air and sea temperatures slowly increased.

Today this is having **disastrous effects.**

Melting ice caps and glaciers, plus the greater volume of warm water, mean sea levels are rising.

Whole countries may disappear as a result.*

Warmer oceans mean storms and hurricanes happen more often and are more powerful.

Rising air temperatures are causing droughts and increasing the size of deserts around the world.

*Tuvalu, Kiribati and the Maldives are all in danger of being swamped.

# Glossary

**Aboriginal Australian** descendant of the original peoples of Australia, who lived there before Europeans arrived

**accretion** in space, the process of matter gathering together in layers to form a planet

**active** volcano that still erupts regularly

**atmosphere** layer of gases around a planet

**break** of a wave, this means the moment when the wave pitches forward and becomes frothy and foamy

**continent** large, continuous area of land; Earth's continents are Africa, Antarctica, Asia, Australia, Europe, North America and South America

**core** centre or heart of a round object, for example a planet

**epicentre** place on Earth's surface directly above where an earthquake happens

**flammable** able to be easily set alight

**glacier** large, solid mass of ice, rock and soil that collects in a steep-sided valley

**ice cap** large areas of ice at the North and South Poles

**magma** liquid or semi-liquid rock from beneath the Earth's crust

**moisture** water contained in air

**parched** dry, without water

**spring** place where water rises up from beneath the ground

**supercell storm** rare kind of giant, violent thunderstorm

**swamped** flooded with water

**tectonic plate** huge section of rock that makes up part of the Earth's outer crust

**tension** strain or stretch that results from two forces being in opposition to each other

**tornado** swirling column of air that can pick up large objects, rip off house roofs and cause lots of damage

**volume** amount of space something takes up

# Finding out more

## Planet Earth places

**The Natural History Museum**
Cromwell Road
London SW7 5BD

The museum has a permanent volcanoes and earthquakes exhibit, which includes models of the bodies of the victims of Mt Vesuvius in CE 79 and modern ways of building an earthquake-resistant house. Another exhibit, Restless Surface, shows how wind, water and weather have helped shape the Earth.

**The Science Museum**
Exhibition Road
London
SW7 2DD

The museum's Atmosphere exhibit on Level 2 offers the chance to explore how Earth's atmosphere works, the ways in which it is changing and the effects of these changes.

## Planet Earth books

*The Big Bang and Beyond* Michael Bright (Wayland, 2016)
Amazing photographs plus 3D graphics explain the Big Bang, the event that gave birth to the Universe, the solar system and planet Earth itself. Part of a series called *Planet Earth* that also has titles on *Early Life On Earth* and *The Evolution Of You And Me*.

*The Big Countdown: Seven Quintillion, Five hundred Quadrillion Grains of Sand on Planet Earth* Paul Rockett (Franklin Watts, 2014)
Starting with the 200 tredecillion atoms in the Earth's atmosphere, progressing through the nine trillion litres of water a hurricane can drop in a day, and finishing with the one core at the centre of the Earth, this book is a number-based collection of fascinating planet Earth facts.

*World in Infographics: Planet Earth* Jon Richards (Wayland, 2013)
Once you start digging into this book, it's hard to stop. From meteorite crashes to exploding volcanoes, the longest rivers to the highest mountains, *Planet Earth* is jammed with fun and fascinating information in an easy-to-explore visual format.

# Index

# Cause Effect and Chaos!

## Titles in this series:

### In the Animal Kingdom

### In Engineering and Industry

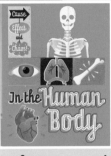

### In the Human Body

### In Outer Space

### In the Rainforest

### On Planet Earth